Jochen Adler

Examining Contributions to a Corporate Microblog as a Bas
System

GRIN - Verlag für akademische Texte

Der GRIN Verlag mit Sitz in München hat sich seit der Gründung im Jahr 1998 auf die Veröffentlichung akademischer Texte spezialisiert.

Die Verlagswebseite www.grin.com ist für Studenten, Hochschullehrer und andere Akademiker die ideale Plattform, ihre Fachtexte, Studienarbeiten, Abschlussarbeiten oder Dissertationen einem breiten Publikum zu präsentieren.

Document Nr. V196182

Jochen Adler

Examining Contributions to a Corporate Microblog as a Basis for an Employee Incentive System

GRIN Verlag

Bibliografische Information der Deutschen Nationalbibliothek: Die Deutsche Bibliothek verzeichnet diese Publikation in der Deutschen Nationalbibliografie; detaillierte bibliografische Daten sind im Internet über http://dnb.d-nb.de/ abrufbar.

1. Auflage 2012
Copyright © 2012 GRIN Verlag GmbH
http://www.grin.com
Druck und Bindung: Books on Demand GmbH, Norderstedt Germany
ISBN 978-3-656-22607-9

AKAD
Private University

Bachelor Thesis
BSWIN

Examining
Contributions to a Corporate Microblog
as a Basis for an Employee Incentive System

Jochen Adler

Langen, May 18th 2012

Abstract

Social media and social networks seem to be conquering human relationships. Corporations are increasingly expecting business benefits from
such platforms for employee-to-employee networking and internal collaboration. But firstly, social software platforms have to be introduced
into an organization successfully, which often requires strategic and cul-
tural changes before the new technology effectively supports everyday
work tasks and corporate procedures. Companies will thus be looking for
ways to promote usage of the new platforms and influence employee behavior accordingly.

After a review of selected relevant scientific theory and practical examples for social software analysis, this thesis analyzes employee contributions to a corporate microblogging platform in order to find a metric for
organizationally desired behaviors. The nature of microblogging – short
text messages that propagate across a network by means of very basic
mechanisms, like *subscription*, *repeats* or *responses* – seems very well
suited for such an analysis. Two metrics, describing an employees' *influence* across the network and the *utility* of their contributions as recognized by peers, were combined in a single numerical score. Such scoring
could be used as a factor within an employee incentive system intended
to reward extraordinarily active or useful contributors.

Acknowledgments

I would like to thank my professors, many of whom have given me new perspectives on facts I thought I had already known from 15 years of practical experience. Especially, Prof. Paul Kirchberg and Prof. Frank Lehmann, who are inspiring teachers and then thankfully made themselves available to supervise my final seminar paper and this Thesis.

At my workplace, Allison, Gerit, John and Thomas have been instrumental in providing the data that became the basis for my research. Philipp deserves thanks for a thorough review of my writing at short notice and during evening hours. Oliver was very helpful as a sparring partner for developer tools and SQL syntax and semantics. Brigitte, Charlotte, Katharina, Miriam, Felix, Jürgen, Heiko and Klaus have helped provide the methodical link between the data set and desired employee behavior. I have lost count of the inspirations I received from talking with colleagues near and far about the possibilities and limitations of social software in the workplace. Obviously, every single notice that our colleagues posted to the microblog has contributed to the findings I could make. Everyone's engagement on the new medium is sincerely appreciated.

Both my parents have been tremendously helpful as proofreaders and, maybe less obviously, as role models and sources for the inspiration and energy required to stay the course towards the completion of an academic degree.

Finally, I owe deepest thanks to my wife Anna. She was the impetus. Now I can look back at a five years attending college besides my regular work, evenings and weekends absent from our family. Considering the amount of changes in our lives that we chose to make during all the while, her warmth, her love and her practical support every day have

facilitated every outcome, from the smallest course examination to this final thesis. I feel like my humble academic accomplishments so far are also hers. It's a deep, intentional, mutual dependency. It's the most permanent, indestructible link imaginable between two humans.

Table of Contents

Table of Figures

List of Abbreviations

API	Application Programming Interface
AJAX	Asynchronous JavaScript and XML
BBC	British Broadcasting Corporation
CIS	Composite Incentive Score
DNS	Domain Name System
FTP	File Transfer Protocol
FV	Favorite feature
HT	Hashtag usage
HTML	Hypertext Markup Language
ID	Identification
INF	Influence Metric
IPO	Initial Public Offering
IT	Information Technology
PC	Personal Computer
RE	Reply feature
RP	Repost feature
RSS	Real Simple Syndication
SQL	Structured Query Language
TAM	Technology Acceptance Model
TCP/IP	Transmission Control Protocol / Internet Protocol
TV	Television
U.K.	United Kingdom of Great Britain and Northern Ireland
U.S.	United States of America
UTAUT	Unified Theory of Acceptance and Use of Technology
UTI	Utility Metric
WWW	World Wide Web
XML	eXtensible Markup Language
XSLT	eXtensible Stylesheet Language Transformation

1   Introduction

Social media and social networks seem to be conquering human relation-ships. The most prominent example, Facebook, is strongly growing to-wards a user base of one billion people all across the planet. At the time of this writing, Facebook is going public, valuing the company at an esti-mated US$ 107 billion, making it the third-largest *initial public offering* (IPO) in U.S. corporate history and the largest IPO ever in the technology sector[1]. People use smartphones with mobile applications to access Face-book and countless other *social* platforms – Twitter, Google+, LinkedIn, Groupon, Foursquare, to name a few – any time and from everywhere: on vacation, from home, at work, or from the commutes in-between. The underlying technology, called *social software*, provides intuitive, easy-to-use interfaces, inviting contributions from and encouraging dialog among participants. People use it to form communities and maintain relation-ships online, establishing an entirely new generation of *socio-technical systems*.

Corporations are increasingly expecting business benefits from such plat-forms for employee-to-employee networking, enabling virtual teamwork and cross-divisional communities of practice or to improve internal com-munications, organizational learning, problem solving and enterprise knowledge management. Before any of those benefits can be harvested, however, social software platforms have to be introduced into an organi-zation successfully. Such an initiative will often require strategic and cul-tural changes before the new spirit of collaboration seamlessly integrates with everyday work tasks and corporate procedures.

Since the success of social software is, by nature, dependent on broad adoption and the quality of employee contributions, companies will be looking for ways to promote usage of the new platforms and influence employee behavior accordingly. Now that the first corporate implementa-tions of social software are available and adoption is progressing, it

---

[1]   http://money.cnn.com/2012/05/17/technology/facebook-ipo-final-price/index.htm

seems promising to define desired employee behaviors and then analyze whether the variety of individual contributions collected on this kind of software platform can be used to find actual evidence of these behaviors.

1.1 Thesis

The following thesis was formulated to guide the research effort:

> „An analysis of content in a corporate microblog provides a measurement of desired employee behavior that can be used in an incentive system to encourage active use and promote technology adoption".

This research paper will attempt to confirm this thesis empirically. It uses a data set derived from an actual corporate microblogging implementation.

1.2 Document Structure

Before detailing the empirical data analysis in chapters 6 and 7, this paper presents the emerging theoretical foundations for the corporate use of microblogging in particular and social software in general (chapter 2). Furthermore, a short literature survey introduces the scientific theory behind corporate change management, corporate strategy and the role of employee incentive systems for strategic alignment (chapter 3). Another short chapter (4) examines the analytics commonly used to measure the success of traditional media, by analogy. Some practical examples of social network analysis (5) shall round off the academic survey.

2   Social Software and Enterprise 2.0

Microblogging is a rather new phenomenon. In March 2006, for example, the now omnipresent social networking service Facebook introduced a feature allowing its users to share brief *status updates* among their friends. July the same year, the dedicated microblogging service Twitter was launched[2]. Twitter is now immensely popular, its name being *de-facto* synonymous to *microblogging* in popular perception. Adoption of the Twitter service is seemingly ever-growing[3]. Due to the intensity of innovation in this area, the object of investigation changes rapidly and scientific analysis becomes relatively difficult.

Meanwhile, however, there seems to be a broad consensus to classify microblogging as a *social* technology (a *social medium* or, more generally, *social software*), and, as such, as a *Web 2.0* phenomenon. Since this research examines the use of microblogging in a corporate context, it is also necessary to present a definition of *Enterprise 2.0*, an umbrella term that has been coined to characterize business applications of Web 2.0 technology and principles. For the purpose of this treatment, it thus seems practical to define these categories – Web 2.0, social software, Enterprise 2.0 – prior to examining microblogging as a specific technique.

2.1   The Web 2.0

The term *Web 2.0* is quite frequently used, but controversial. In a stricter sense, Web 2.0 is not a scientific definition, but rather the outcome of a brainstorming with practitioners[4]: At an industry conference in 2005, attendants were asked to name novel, remarkably successful internet services since the burst of the *dot-com bubble* in 2001. A broad, seemingly diverse range of contributions arose, but upon closer examination, there were also striking similarities.

---

[2] http://www.twitter.com; cf. [Naon08] as well as [Koch09] p. 35
[3] cf. [Java07]
[4] cf. [ORei05]

On the one hand, all those Internet offerings were broadly soliciting and encouraging *contributions from their users*, allowing participation while not requiring the possession of any technical skills[5]. On the other hand, and by contrast to traditional web software, they seemed to *facilitate the combination of data from various sources* and applications from various areas[6] in an open fashion and in a rather playful way[7]. Another common characteristic of Web 2.0 applications is their *openness with respect to the data and services* that they provide: In many cases, application programming interfaces (APIs) were provided for unrestricted access, spawning unforeseen, creative uses; allowing the consumption of those services on a wide range of devices[8] and operating system platforms[9].

Resulting from the heuristic definition, arguably, the term Web 2.0 does not seem to be used and understood consistently[10]. The choice of terminology could in fact be criticized: Contrary to what the analogy to a software product's version number (*2.0*) suggests, no upgrade or enhancement of WWW technology is involved[11]. Technological advances in fact play only a marginal role to constitute this *new generation* of Internet services: The underlying innovations[12] are supplements or enhancements of conventional Web technology.

2.2 Social Software

An apparently more precise term than Web 2.0 is *social software*[13]. "Social software applications are supporting, as part of a *socio-technical* system, human communication, interaction and collaboration. The actors are thereby leveraging the potential and contributions of a network of active

---

[5] such as knowing how to create HTML documents or using FTP for transferring content
[6] the term "mash-up" emerged to describe the presentation of any new combination of information from originally distinct sources
[7] cf. [Buhs09], p. 66
[8] e.g. originally on PCs with web browsers, but then also on smartphones
[9] cf. [Koch09], p. 3
[10] cf. [Back08], p. 3
[11] e.g. TCP/IP, DNS, or HTTP
[12] e.g. technologies like Web Services, AJAX, RSS or XSLT should be mentioned
[13] Even this term, however, is not free from critique: The connotation that "social" activities are also "leisure" activities (i.e. non-work) can be inappropriate (cf. [McAf09] p. 16f).

participants."[14] In this definition, the idea of a system in both the *social* and the *technical* senses is crucial: The active inclusion and utilization of *participant contributions* is the single most important characteristic for social software.

For an early example of how an application of this principle has significantly influenced the course of Internet history, let us look at Google's *PageRank* algorithm[15]: With Page Rank, priority for any given search result does not at all depend on attributes of the page in question, but rather on the *quality and number of links from other, external documents* to the page in question. PageRank effectively applied the technique of academic citation to Internet search[16]. Rather than considering the properties of the web content itself, the new algorithm assessed how *other contributions* considered its relevance (assuming that hyperlinks are only placed to content that is considered relevant). PageRank, in essence, was based on *relationships* between web pages rather than their content. Building on this idea, Google could deliver better and more useful search results than any other Internet search engine at the time[17]: With the introduction of PageRank, search rankings were much harder to manipulate.

Nowadays, the social software principle is reaching a lot further. There are countless practical examples of platforms built around substantial contributions from participants, in the Internet as well as for internal corporate use (Intranet). The most popular and successful Internet example for a service built upon community contributions, arguably, is *Wikipedia*[18], but there are also examples of corporate Intranet platforms based on Wiki software to provide collections of employee knowledge[19].

---

[14] [Back09], p. 1; author's translation
[15] see [Page04]
[16] cf. [Pari11]
[17] cf. [McAf09], p. 63ff
[18] see http://en.wikipedia.org
[19] cf. [Koch09], p. 37ff

2.3   Enterprise 2.0

By analogy to Web 2.0, elements of corporate strategies that build on user-generated content and social software platforms for business benefit are termed *Enterprise 2.0*.

According to Michael Koch and Alexander Richter, Enterprise 2.0 is about "comprehending the concepts behind Web 2.0 and social software, and attempting to transfer and apply them to collaboration in enterprises"[20]. Corporations embrace the new paradigm and hope for better business performance because there is "the observation that established corporate infrastructures do no longer live up to the requirements of knowledge work. [...] It is seen as a central management task to provide easy access to the implicit know-how, experience and ideas of knowledge workers"[21].

Because, as we saw, social software is a socio-technical system, success-fully establishing an Enterprise 2.0 work environment is more dependent on human factors than on technical features[22]. The openness that comes with social software presents challenges to corporate management. The free flow of information, irrespective of traditional organizational or hier-archical boundaries, threatens to dilute authority, requiring new leader-ship styles and demanding new leader qualifications and behaviors. Grown up with digital devices and naturally accustomed to Internet tech-nology, young professionals are now *high potentials* in a time where demographic change puts the supply for talent under additional pres-sure[23]. The literature review in chapter 3 will provide more detail on theo-ries examining corporate change management, corporate strategy and strategic alignment.

2.4   Microblogs and Microblogging

A *microblog* is a specific breed of social software that allows its users to exchange short messages with potentially any other user of the platform.

---

[20] [Koch09], p. 16; author's translation
[21] [Back09], p. 23; author's translation
[22] cf. foreword by Andrew McAfee to [Buhs08], p. 1
[23] cf. [Buhs08]

Such messages can be sent and received from a wide variety of devices and irrespective of location, on *personal computers*, on conventional mobile phones[24], or on Internet-connected smartphones. Each participant can observe a constant stream of messages on the platform by *following* (subscribing to) the contributions of any number of other users at their own liberty, thereby effectively configuring their own personal stream of news updates that the platform then presents to them in strictly chronological order[25]. Participants can interact with other users' messages, so that information travels across the network and conversation threads can emerge. Using the Twitter service as an example, it is possible for the recipient of any microblog communication to

- respond to the message (*reply*), commencing or advancing dialog
- spread the message further (*retweet*), exposing the content to a wider audience
- mark the message as useful (*favorite*), recognizing the original contribution as valuable.

Twitter is designed for maximum speed and simplicity: Each of these interactions takes users of the service only a single mouse click.

---

[24] Twitter is limiting messages to 140 characters purposefully, so that they can be composed and transmitted as cell phone text messages via the SMS protocol
[25] Because of its chronological order, the resulting stream of updates is called the "timeline"

Fig. 1:   Twitter's "timeline", including menu of actions (reply, retweet, favorite)

The entire dialog takes place in public – any user can subscribe to any other user's messages – unless specific privacy settings are put in place by one of the parties in conversation. The verb used to describe activity on a microblog platform is *microblogging.*

Contrary to what the name might suggest, microblogging is actually closer in nature to *instant messaging* (*chat*) than to blogging[26]. Due to the fact that updating one's microblog takes significantly less time than writing a contribution to one's blog, microbloggers typically update their status several times per day, whereas bloggers only publish new articles once every few days[27]. The possibility to compose messages from any-where, independently of location, e.g. via cell phone text messages or from smartphone, has added to the popularity of microblogging.

After Twitter's immense success, other significant social or professional networking sites have given their users possibilities to keep their contacts informed with short, regular status updates[28]. Unlike other social soft-ware technologies, especially Wikis and Blogs, however, microblogging does not seem to be widely recognized as a technique for professional or corporate use.

---

[26] cf. [Koch09], p. 36
[27] cf. [Java07]
[28] "share an update" (LinkedIn), "message" (Xing), cf. [Koch09], p. 36

2.5   Corporate Uses for Microblogging

An increasing number of commercial microblogging implementations is available to corporations, either as an Internet-based *cloud service* (e.g. Yammer[29], Communote[30]), or as a specific feature of an Intranet-based collaboration platform (e.g. Jive[31], Blogtronix[32], JustConnect[33]). Moreover, the established providers of enterprise software (like customer relationship, sales force management or collaboration infrastructure solutions) are also adding microblogging features to their suites (e.g. Saleforce Chatter[34], Tibco Tibbr[35]). It can thus be said with certainty that there is a considerable supply of microblogging solutions in support of business processes and business operations[36].

Several recent examples have highlighted singular cases where microblogging was put to business use, most notably related to internal communications, knowledge management, employee social networking and collaboration. An impressive collection of respective cases has been compiled by a group of scientists from the Universität der Bundeswehr Munich and St. Gallen University, featuring, most notably, studies of examples from CapGemini[37], Communardo[38] and Siemens Building Solutions[39].

From a perspective of teamwork in software engineering, a notable study has highlighted the potential of social software, including microblogs, to enable "new ways for software teams to form and work together"[40].

Examining project management and project teamwork, the possibility of using a microblog for communication on distributed virtual teams and as

---

[29] https://www.yammer.com
[30] http://www.communote.com
[31] http://www.jivesoftware.com
[32] http://www.blogtronix.com
[33] http://www.justsoftwareag.com
[34] http://www.salesforce.com/chatter
[35] http://www.tibbr.com/
[36] see also [News10]
[37] http://www.e20cases.org/fallstudie/capgemini-microblogging-als-konversationsmedium/
[38] http://www.e20cases.org/fallstudie/communardo-software-gmbh-enterprise-microblogging/
[39] http://www.e20cases.org/fallstudie/siemens-building-technologies-division-globaler-wissens-und-erfahrungsaustausch-mit-references-2/
[40] cf. [Bege10]

an alternative to e-mail, has been described in an earlier study by the author of this thesis[41].

2.6   Adoption and Change

Social software relies on contributions from a broad range of individuals. In order to successfully introduce a social software platform into an enterprise, employees must participate in a change effort that affects their attitudes and behaviors rather fundamentally: Where they were previously used to *consume* data and information passively, e.g. browsing the news stories on a static corporate intranet, they will now have to become more engaged, acting not only as consumers, but also as *producers* or *publishers* of content. That's why the following chapters will present an overview of theories behind organizational change and incentive systems to motivate the individual and on the evolution of publishing from Gutenberg's printing press to user-generated content.

---

[41] cf. [Adle11]

3   Change Management and Incentives

There seems to be a broad consensus supporting the statement that corporations generally are under stronger pressure today to react and adapt
to the dynamics of their market environment – hence, to *change* – than
they were a decade or a generation of leaders ago. As one source[42]
points out, "with less global competition and a slower-moving business
environment, the norm back then was stability and the ruling motto was
if it ain't broke, don't fix it". Before reviewing scientific theory around
corporate change, the next section will elaborate how the *globalization of
markets and competition* since the 1990s has been, on the one hand, a
source of hazards (more competitors and an increased speed of competition), but also, on the other hand, a source of opportunity (bigger markets with fewer barriers).

Arguably, the forces of globalization do not apply equally to all sorts of
enterprises: A corporation in a regional market, dealing with material
goods and physical products, may well be under less pressure to change
than a global corporation dealing with immaterial goods or services such
as media or information. Given the specific object of this study, though, it
is necessary to emphasize the global economic environment: The microblogging platform examined in chapters 6 and 7 was implemented at a
global corporation with employees in over 70 countries. In such a business environment, the particular challenges of the *information age* –
strategic alignment, knowledge management and virtual teamwork – certainly operate most forcefully. That is why we begin by introducing globalization as a phenomenon before looking more specifically at corporate
change, management by objectives, the balanced scorecard, technology
adoption models and corporate incentive systems.

---

[42] [Kott96], p. 18

3.1 Globalization

John P. Kotter identifies four major factors that have been driving what is more generally referred to as globalization[43]:

1. Technological change (faster and better communication, faster and better transportation, more information networks connecting people globally)
2. International economic integration (fewer tariffs, currencies linked via floating exchange rates, more global capital flow)
3. Maturation of markets in developed countries (slower domestic growth, more aggressive exporters, more deregulation)
4. Fall of communist and socialist regimes (more countries linked to the capitalist system, more privatization).

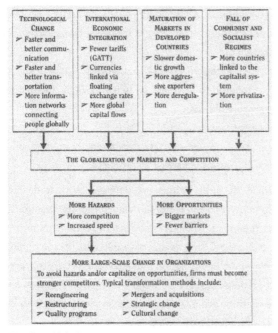

Fig. 2:   Globalization Hazards and Opportunities (from [Kott96], p. 19)

A more contemporary source[44] cites three major reasons why corporations and their strategic leadership have been under pressure to change faster and more drastically in the first decade of the 21st century:

1. Globalization
2. A new quality of competition through new forms of collaboration between enterprises (partnerships, networks)
3. New communication technologies.

Speaking of the post-cold-war global economy as the *information age*, Norton and Kaplan[45] state that organizations are now "built on a new set of operating assumptions", namely:

1. Cross-functions: integrated business processes that cut across traditional business functions.
2. Links to customers and suppliers: integrating supply, production and delivery so that operations are triggered by customer orders, not production plans.
3. Customer segmentation: offering customized products and services that can be tailored to a variety of demands while still being produced at reasonable cost.
4. Global scale (as seen above).
5. Innovation: shrinking product life cycles require continuous improvement in processes as well as products.

Interestingly, while the three sources use different terms to describe the economic environment and the factors driving corporate change, they all clearly point out the *influence of technological developments* and the role of *information technology*. So it seems plausible that microblogging – as the introduction of a new information management paradigm, turning consumers into producers (see 4.5) and providing new features for the diffusion of information (see 5.5) – is an appropriate example to illustrate the necessity for organizational change.

---

[44] cf. [Hahn06], preface to the 6th edition, p. IX
[45] [Nort96], p. 4f

3.2   Organizational Change Management (according to John P. Kotter)

Scientists examining and describing how organizations react to changing competitive environments have concluded that organizational change is a complex subject. Not only do processes and systems require redesign and improvement, but individuals with their variety of personalities have to be *aligned*, or even inspired, to follow a common vision and a set of goals supporting the desired changes. John P. Kotter, for example, has distilled his research into a generic eight-stage model for an organizational change process[46]:

1. Establishing a Sense of Urgency
2. Creating the Guiding Coalition
3. Developing a Vision and Strategy
4. Communicating the Change Vision
5. Empowering Employees for Broad-Based Action
6. Generating Short-Term Wins
7. Consolidating Gains and Producing More Change
8. Anchoring New Approaches in the Culture

Several stages in this process seem to underline the importance to reach out to a broad base of employees in order to solidify the change. Examining one example of an unsuccessful transformation initiative from a *human resources* perspective, for example, Kotter found out that[47]:

- performance evaluation forms captured nothing about the core of the new vision
- compensation decisions were made much more on not making mistakes than on creating useful change
- promotion decisions seemed to have at best a limited relationship to the desired change effort
- recruiting and hiring systems were only marginally supporting the transformation

---

[46] see [Kott96]
[47] cf. [Kott96], p. 110f

Irrespective of the specific example under examination, this list is a good summary of four major general characteristics in any human resources management system or process that can be designed to either support or hinder organizational changes: performance evaluation, compensation, promotions, recruiting/hiring.

Human resources management systems and processes that spell out and actively support the goal of the change process are also critical when it comes to anchor the new approach in the culture of the organization for the long term. If any change is to be sustainable without constant extra investments and efforts, then, at some point, the successful new behaviors and practices have to become firmly rooted and incorporated in the corporate culture. This will make the organization less dependent on individual contributions and should help preserve the desired behaviors over generations of employees, even if key people retire, or in times of increased turnover[48].

In order to accomplish such long-term sustainability, desired behaviors have to be recognized (performance evaluation) and ideally rewarded (compensation). People who successfully model the desired change have to be supported in their careers (ideally promoted), and new employees entering the workforce should be selected based on criteria that support the goals of the change effort (recruiting/hiring).

These requirements towards human resource management systems and processes deserve emphasis: As *socio-technical* systems, their success is dependent on human factors more than technical capability. But how can all this be accomplished while recognizing the complexity of today's global business environment for a multi-national corporation? Long-standing theories can be helpful, especially management by objectives, the balanced scorecard and – since we are specifically interested in the adoption of an information system – technology acceptance models.

---

[48] cf. [Kott96], p. 145ff

3.3   Management By Objectives (according to Peter F. Drucker)

Changing organizational demands require carefully adjusted objectives. Especially during periods of change, objectives that are properly broken down and tied to the goals of the desired organizational transformation can provide a powerful management instrument to lead employees through uncertainty and turbulence[49]. The fundamental management theory, however, is much older, predating globalization and the notion of *Enterprise 2.0* by decades.

Peter F. Drucker pointed out as early as 1956[50] that corporations must be able to successfully combine individual efforts. Any member of the organization will contribute specifically and uniquely, but a contribution towards a collective, common goal is also required, and from anyone. All efforts have to be aligned in a common direction to create a whole – without gaps, without friction, without unnecessary redundancy[51].

Based on this ideal, he developed the concept of *managing by objectives* that has long become a de facto standard in larger corporations[52].

When managing by objectives, a manager will formulate objectives for each individual contributor that are at the same time motivating and traceably supporting the overall goals of the corporation. Two problems can arise: linking individual contributions to corporate strategy is often difficult or even impossible if not supported by a process (see the next section on the balanced scorecard), and there seems to be a common lack of feedback between managers and employees for the principle to work practically[53].

---

[49] cf. [Dopp08], p. 288
[50] he actually wrote his hallmark book in 1954, but the only source available was a German-language edition from 1956
[51] [Druc56], p. 153
[52] according to [Dörf12], p. 56
[53] [Dörf12], p. 56

To function effectively, it is said that objectives should be stated as clearly (or *hard*) as possible, being[54]

- specific,
- measurable,
- attainable,
- relevant, and
- time-bound.

By contrast, statements of goals that are not specific or less measurable are commonly called *soft* objectives and sometimes dismissed or neglected. Considering employee use of *information systems*, however, employee behavior seems fairly suitable for objective setting and performance management, because these systems and their digital records are *measurable and specific* by nature.

3.4 Balanced Scorecard (according to Kaplan and Norton)

Fourty years after Drucker's initial introduction of objective-based management and leadership, Robert S. Kaplan and David P. Norton introduced the *balanced scorecard*, summarizing it as a concept to "translate strategy into action"[55] and noting that "an organization's measurement system strongly affects the behavior of people both inside and outside the organization"[56].

Kaplan and Norton point out that, historically, the measurement of business has been financial, to a degree that financial success and business success are often understood synonymously. They also reaffirm that it is important to install and maintain measurement systems[57] which allow fact-based and informed decision-making while eliminating unnecessary factors of personal taste, or individual temper, or short-term mood.

---

[54] according to [Dörf12], p. 56f and other sources
[55] [Kapl96] book subtitle
[56] [Kapl96], p. 21
[57] their phrase "if you can't measure it, you can't manage it" ([Kapl96], p. 21) has become a managerial bon-mot

In the area of corporate financial performance, measurability may seem natural, because a *currency* exists to express success or failure precisely (e.g. based on *cash flow variation*, *operational profitability margin*, or *return on equity*). Far less obviously, though, their theory demands that not only financial performance should be measured. Instead, they suggest a more *balanced* approach that weighs in performance indicators relating to business performance with respect to *customer satisfaction*, *business process efficiency* as well as *organizational learning and growth*. Their framework suggests that specific indicators should be defined – unambiguously stated objectives along with measurements, targets, and specifically named initiatives like transformation projects – for each of these areas, effectively translating corporate strategy into operational terms. Ideally, all the objectives stated in the balanced score card can be formulated along with *performance indicators* – items of information collected at regular intervals to track the performance of a system[58]. Based on such scoring, the corporation can *measure* whether any objective has been exceeded, met or missed.

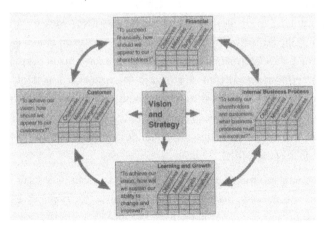

Fig. 3:   Model of the "Balanced Scorecard" (from [Kapl96], p. 9)

---

[58] cf. [Fitz90]

Kaplan and Norton realized that there often was "a large void between the [corporate] mission statement and employees' day-to-day actions"[59]. Focusing on measurability while at the same time taking a broader view beyond mere financials, the balanced scorecard intends to translate the high-level vision and mission for an organization into guidance for employees on all levels. The model aims to be practical and applicable in everyday situations. It is intended as a "communication, informing and learning system, not a controlling system"[60].

3.5 Technology Acceptance Models

In the 1980s, with computer hardware prices steadily decaying and the arrival of the *personal computer*, information systems were becoming increasingly common in the workplace. A new generation of systems emerged, defined by Fred D. Davis as "systems that are directly used by organizational members at their own discretion and support their work activities". They were therefore labeled *end-user systems*[61].

Davis pointed out that while it was clearly recognized that computers were a driving economical force and end-user systems were going to be economically attractive, investment decisions and design alternatives concerning new information systems were commonly made based on objective performance criteria. He criticized shortcomings in understanding the more subtle subjective factors that could determine whether end-users would broadly accept and actually utilize the new system for everyday tasks. In response to this challenge, he developed the *Technology Acceptance Model* (TAM).

Davis' model has motivated system designers to continually focus on end-user needs when building software (including, for example, early prototyping and standardized testing). Because of the rapid pace of innovation, designing technology so that the intended users will accept them remains a very relevant topic to the present day. Directly involving end-

---

[59] [Kapl96], p. 25
[60] [Kapl96], p. 25
[61] [Davi86], p. 9

users in the process[62], for example, can help significantly to accomplish *usefulness* and *ease of use*.

The model was later combined with other models describing information technology acceptance in an attempt to unify the discipline (by Venkatesh et. al.). The resulting universal model is called *Unified Theory of Acceptance and Use of Technology* (UTAUT). Most notably for the purpose of this research, UTAUT incorporated *social influence* as one of the factors contributing to an individual's acceptance of a new technology[63].

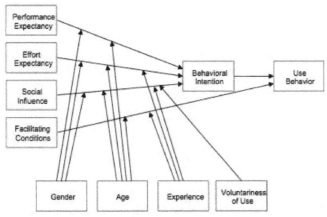

Fig. 4:   Unified Theory of Acceptance and Use of Technology (visualization)[64]

With social software systems, however, the concept of *usefulness* seems to depend less immediately on the actual design characteristics of the system or platform applied. Social software, instead, draws much of its value to the individual from the breadth and depth of contributions from others in the community of platform users. One recent analysis[65] recognizes this circumstance by proposing modifications to the UTAUT that are specific to microblogging for corporate purposes.

---

[62] cf. [Abra04]
[63] cf. [Venk03], p. 452
[64] [Venk03], p. 447
[65] cf. [Günt09], p. 3; note that the source examines the enterprise use of Twitter as opposed to the enterprise use of an internal (Intranet-based) microblogging platform

That is why, leading back to the central question of this research paper, in order to enhance the *perceived usefulness* of a social software platform to the individual, it should be examined how well the system has already been adopted by others in the organization. If necessary, adoption can be promoted by means of an *incentive system*.

3.6   Strategic Alignment and Incentive Systems

If a corporation is hoping that strategic benefit can be gained from lever-aging social software[66], it will be looking for ways to motivate managers and individual contributors alike to support its introduction. For social software specifically, current research seems to suggest a relatively strong correlation between the ability to successfully integrate the tech-nology into employees' everyday workflows and positive corporate results (made evident by considering metrics like *return on sales*).[67]

The desired state of consistency between strategic objectives and opera-tional day-to-day procedures is called *strategic alignment* according to Kaplan and Norton: "By communicating the strategy and by linking it to personal goals, all organizational efforts and initiatives can become aligned to the needed transformation processes."[68] Among corporations with effective strategic alignment, Kaplan and Norton identified three mechanisms that were often combined successfully: (1) communication and education, (2) management by objectives, and (3) the linkage of de-sired employee behavior to a corporate *reward system*, which leads us back to the thesis at the center of this analysis.

Some research has come to the conclusion that variable payment is an effective agent when used as part of a wider organizational change strat-egy[69]. Taking a broader view, though, a corporate reward system (or *in-centive system*) may or may not provide financial rewards. It may at-tempt to link employee behavior to corporate strategy by using explicit, predetermined formulas, but it may also be applied judgmentally. Dis-

---

[66]   current surveys seem to suggest that this is in fact true, cf. [Bugh11]
[67]   [Dörf12], p. 53
[68]   [Kapl96], p. 200
[69]   [Belc96], p. 14

cussing the role of incentive systems for strategic alignment, Kaplan and Norton argue that "the question is not whether, but when and how the connection should be made"[70].

---

[70] [Kapl96], p. 217

4   Conventional Media and Media Reception

In the next chapter, some practical examples of social software analytics and the theory of information diffusion in social networks will take us to the essential purpose of this research: Mining the contributions to a corporate microblog for material that might be useful in designing incentive systems and supporting the alignment of individual behavior with business strategy. But beforehand, this chapter will be a short excursus examining how the success and reception of traditional media can be measured.

4.1   Print Media

With the revolutionary invention of the printing press by Johannes Gutenberg in the 15th century, the age of publishing began[71]. Since then, publications via books, daily newspapers and periodical magazines have reached audiences in large numbers. Especially because newspapers and magazines are advertising media (and advertisers want proof that their budget is well spent), a lot of practical effort is put into determining the success of a periodical publication; in Germany, for example, a publishing industry advocacy group provides regular market research.[72]

The most commonly used metrics are *circulation* (German: 'Auflage') and *reach* ('Reichweite'). While *circulation* expresses how many copies of the printed medium are sold (either individually or as regular subscriptions), *reach* attempts to measure by how many consumers the content in the medium is actually read. There is certainly very interesting empirical science behind this metric[73], but a more detailed treatment would go well beyond the scope of this research.

---

[71] http://en.wikipedia.org/wiki/Publishing
[72] see e.g. http://www.vdz.de/uploads/media/Branchendaten_PZ_2011.pdf.pdf
[73] the analyisis for 2006 was based on 39,000 individual interviews, see
     http://de.wikipedia.org/wiki/Deutsche_Media-Analyse#MA_Pressemedien

4.2 Broadcast Media

Television and radio also are *mass media*, where content is produced and provided with the intention of reaching large audiences. This seems to make them equally attractive for advertising. Determining the success of broadcasts, however, is even harder than for print media: The technical devices are operated by consumers (TV sets, radio receivers) and can be tuned in to a variety of programs. There is no technical possibility to determine when the device was switched on and off or which program it was tuned to. Similar to publishers, the broadcast industry uses empirical analysis to determine the success of their products.

For radio, for example, an analysis based on telephone interviews is used[74], at least in Germany, to determine metrics such as *listeners per hour*, *listeners per day*, or *listeners per average hour*. The U.S. television industry applies a metric known as the *Nielsen ratings*[75]. These scores are based on a representative target audience who either keep records of their viewing habits or have *set meter* devices attached to their TV sets for additional precision. The most important of these metrics are expressed as two key indicators: a program's *rating* (estimating the total number of individual viewers) and *share* (indicating the percentage of TV viewers during the air-time that were tuned in to the particular program).

4.3 The Internet and Website Analytics

The Internet is changing economy and society so quickly and radically that it is difficult to even understand and describe. The traditional media businesses of publishing and broadcasting – and along with them, advertising – are struggling with disruptive changes. Following sections of this chapter will describe only two of the driving forces, because of their direct relevance to enterprise microblogging and corporate incentive systems: consumer feedback and user-generated content.

---

[74] the 2006 analysis encompassed interviews with over 58,000 individuals, see
http://de.wikipedia.org/wiki/Deutsche_Media-Analyse#MA_Radio
[75] http://en.wikipedia.org/wiki/Nielsen_ratings

Let us put these new ideas aside for a moment, though, and just look at what the Internet means for the traditional one-way model of content publication and reception. Because the technological foundation of the Internet is digital, it becomes very easy to obtain insights into the success of any web publication[76]. Indicators such as *visitors* to content on the web (roughly the equivalent of print media *reach*) can be expressed with much more precision (e.g. differentiating between *new visitors*, *repeat visitors* and *total unique visitors*). Additionally, much more sophisticated metrics are available for free or at little cost, such as *page view times* or *click paths*.

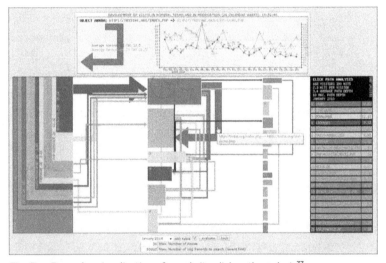

Fig. 5: Example: visualization of a website click path analysis[77]

Services like Alexa[78] can analyze web traffic and provide extremely powerful analytics for free, covering not only visitors and data volumes, but also search engine traffic and even audience demographics.

---

[76] http://en.wikipedia.org/wiki/Web_analytics
[77] http://en.wikipedia.org/wiki/File:Clickpath_Analysis.png
[78] http://www.alexa.com

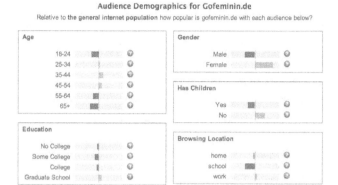

Fig. 6:   Example: website audience demographics for gofeminin.de[79]

4.4   Consumer Feedback and Customer Reviews

Web site analytics have provided a powerful new methodology. They were, however, a truly revolutionary force only quite in the beginning of Internet publishing. Little later, the technological and conceptual advances of the Web 2.0 (see 2.1 above) started to influence businesses even more profoundly: Merchants invited *consumer feedback* on their websites, and customers were now able to publicly express their satisfaction or dissatisfaction in the form of product reviews.

Fig. 7:   Example: consumer feedback on a commerce website[80]

---

[79] http://www.alexa.com/siteinfo/gofeminin.de

Quite obviously, this possibility has opened up an entirely new dimension to analyze the success of any publication. Looking at the example above (a book review from amazon.com), the *customer satisfaction* rating (expressed here as 4.7 stars on a 5-star scale and based on 36 individual customer reviews) now provides a *qualitative* metric that can supplement the *quantitative* indicators used to determine the success of traditional media (such as *circulation* or the amazon.com *sales rank*).

4.5   User-Generated Content, Citizen Journalism and Prosumers

Consumer reviews, in turn, were only a first indicator of a much broader movement towards *user-generated content* on the Internet. One early manifestation of this trend is *citizen journalism*: Following a catastrophic fire in an oil storage terminal in December 2005, the British Broadcasting Corporation (BBC) received over 5,000 photos from viewers and installed a permanent team to receive and incorporate user-generated content into its broadcasts[81].

The Internet is clearly advancing the *democratization of knowledge*: information and opinion can now be published and disseminated without an investment into or even physical access to a printing press. Anyone connected to the Internet can contribute original content, be it in the form of a blog[82], or in the form of images, audio or video[83]. The term *prosumer* has been coined as a contraction of *producer* and *consumer*[84]: Internet users can constantly switch roles between creation and consumption without switching media. The lines between publication and reception have been blurred to an extent where measuring the success of a publication based on *reception* alone – as is the case with print and broadcast media – seems fundamentally insufficient.

---

[80] http://www.amazon.com/Enterprise-2-0-Collaborative-Organizations-Challenges/dp/1422125874/ref=sr_1_1?ie=UTF8&qid=1337260046&sr=8-1
[81] see http://en.wikipedia.org/wiki/User-generated_content#Adoption_and_recognition_by_mass_media
[82] see e.g. http://www.wordpress.com
[83] see e.g. http://www.flickr.com, http://www.soundcloud.com, http://www.youtube.com
[84] Gabler Wirtschaftslexikon, keyword: "prosumer", available online: http://wirtschaftslexikon.gabler.de/Archiv/143860/prosumer-v2.html; *prosumer* has also been defined as a contraction of *professional* and *consumer*

The next chapter will introduce some advanced practical examples for analytics specifically built around user-generated content on social networks.

4.6 Impact

The trend towards user-generated content discussed in this chapter is not only relevant culturally, but also commercially: Scientific analysis now shows that user-generated content influences the products and brands considered for purchase significantly and has profound impacts on purchase decisions.[85]

Looking at the contributions that employees made as *prosumers* on a corporate microblog, it will hopefully become clear that such platforms can provide very interesting metrics that allow not only quantitative, but also *qualitative* judgments and can thus be a factor in designing effective employee incentive systems.

---

[85] cf. [Rieg07]

5 Social Software Analysis and Information Diffusion

Analyzing contributions to a social software platform in masses, in order to derive meaningful metrics, is at the heart of the thesis formulated at the beginning this research. Underlining that this effort is not purely academic, the following sections will try to provide an overview of three practical applications that analyze *traffic* on social media. While these services seem to take distinct, different angles on social software contributions, all have one practical purpose in common: to derive *analytical insights* from the constant flow of contributions, and thereby potentially facilitate or empower business intelligence and business decisions. Furthermore, an introduction to the theory of *information diffusion* should be helpful in understanding how metrics derived from a microblog can support this thesis.

5.1 Klout

Klout seems to be the most influential practical example of social software analysis at present. Klout describes itself[86] as measuring "influence based on [someone's] ability to drive action", adding: "Every time you create content or engage, you influence others." Based on an analysis of an individual's contributions to various social software platforms (Twitter, Facebook, Google+ and LinkedIn, to name a few), Klout calculates an *influence metric* on a scale ranking from 0 to 100 points.

---

[86] http://klout.com/corp/kscore

Fig. 8:   *Klout score for Barack Obama, U.S. President*[87]

The precise algorithm used is proprietary, but Klout discloses that they use three components to calculate what's called the *Klout score*[88]:

1. *True Reach*: The number of people who are acting upon (i.e. responding to or sharing) the individual's contributions to the social network.

2. *Amplification*: The intensity of influence exerted by the participant, i.e. measuring how frequently those members of the individual's network act upon their contributions.

3. *Network*: This component adds a recursive element to the computation of the Kout score. It expresses how influential the people within the individual's *True Reach* are, in turn.

5.2 Socialmention

Socialmention is a search engine, superficially comparable to the widely popular service from Google. With its emphasis on social media sources, though, Socialmention is able to provide not only search results, but also

---

[87] http://klout.com/#/barackobama/score-analysis, screenshot captured on Apr-19 2012
[88] http://klout.com/corp/kscore

certain metrics based on an analysis of contributions by individuals to social media platforms. Socialmention can be used by corporate brands to find out how people are referring to the keywords used in the search.

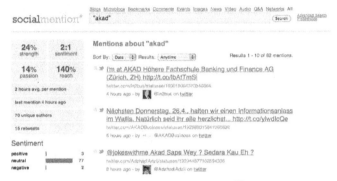

Fig. 9:   Socialmention search results for "AKAD"[89]

Particularly, Socialmention provides the following analytics with respect to a search term queried:

1. *Strength*: An intensity metric, describing the frequency or likelihood that the search term, i.e. a brand name, is mentioned or discussed in social media, expressed as a percentage.

2. *Sentiment*: A relative comparison of those mentions that are generally positive versus those that are generally negative, expressed as a ratio.

3. *Passion*: Another intensity metric, expressing the likelihood that individuals who are mentioning the search term, i.e. a brand name, will do so repeatedly.

4. *Reach*: A measure of the range of influence, computed by putting the total number of unique contributors mentioning the search term, i.e. a brand name, in relation with the total number of mentions overall.

While using similar analytics, Klout and Socialmention pursue opposing objectives: Where Klout attempts to measure the influence on a social

---

[89] http://socialmention.com, screenshot captured on Apr-19 2012

network (individually), Socialmention attempts to capture the *public opin-ion* on a given subject (collectively).

5.3 Facebook Insights

Facebook may mostly be popular for casual social networking, but the platform and its vast base of active users across the globe also provide the basis for an extremely successful business model[90]. Its primary source of income being advertising, Facebook provides advertisers with tools to direct their content to the most relevant target groups and measure the reception of their messages. The ideas introduced in chapter 4 are now taken up again.

Facebook Insights is a powerful suite of several analytical tools. This section illustrates its applicability by example. An exhaustive description would go well beyond the scope of this research.

One example of how the analytics can be used is to look at the *reach* of content posted to the Facebook platform: Insights can report on how often posts are viewed by other Facebook users over time, and differentiate between *organic views* (views by the author's *friends* on the Facebook platform), *paid views* (i.e. clicks on commercially sponsored advertisements) and *viral views* (clicks on content that has been propagated through sharing by the author's Facebook friends to their friends in turn).

---

[90] cf. e.g. "United States Securities and Exchange Commission, Registration Statement, Facebook, Inc.", http://sec.gov/Archives/edgar/data/1326801/000119312512034517/d287954ds1.htm#toc287954_10

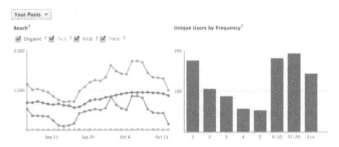

Fig. 10: Facebook Insights, "Reach" and "Unique Users by Frequency" metrics[91]

Since the Facebook platform identifies its users and is thus aware of gender and age, it is possible to provide detailed reporting on the *demographics* of individuals who have *interacted* with the content provided on Facebook (e.g. in the form of posting comments, sharing the message, or clicking the *Like* button). Such analytics express a new dimension in media reception: Where traditional web and print metrics like *reach* quantified the *readers* or *viewers* of content, social media can now provide the basis to quantify the number of *actors* and *doers*.

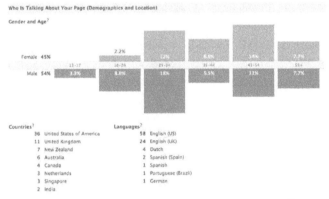

Fig. 11: Facebook Insights, "Who Is Talking About..." metrics[92]

[91] http://www.incomediary.com/wp-content/uploads/2011/10/Screen-shot-2011-10-18-at-13.53.29.png, screenshot captured on Apr-19 2012
[92] http://www.incomediary.com/wp-content/uploads/2011/10/Screen-shot-2011-10-18-at-16.16.41.png, screenshot captured on Apr-19 2012

5.4   Practical Relevance of Klout and Facebook Insights

The metrics based on contributions to social software platforms introduced in this chapter may seem like technical *gimmicks* of little practical
relevance. However, as companies are looking for ways to gain competitive advantage, winning or engaging customers on social media platforms, or aiming to improve sales or service, such analytics are actually
obtaining practical relevance rather quickly.

To give one example, corporations are increasingly engaged as actors on
social media platforms. Initially, their main focus was on distributing corporate news and product or service information: Social media were used
as a *publishing* alternative, challenging traditional advertising and public
relations channels[93]. More recently, though, companies are experiencing
that their customers make use of *consumer feedback opportunities* or
user-generated content to propagate sentiment and opinion on brand
products and services.

Firstly, this trend gives a corporation an opportunity to *analyze* the relevant contributions to these platforms: Monitoring contributions, or using
sentiment analysis to differentiate between positive or negative refer-
ences to the brand, can be a powerful supplement to traditional *market
research*[94]. Adding metrics like Socialmention or Facebook Insights to
such analyses can give marketers additional possibilities to monitor a
brand's image and measure a company's reputation, or to report back on
the effectiveness of more traditional publicity measures such as main-
stream media advertising campaigns.

Secondly, corporations are increasingly seeing social media channels as
an alternative for timely and cost-effective *customer service*[95]. Customer
complaints expressed publicly on social media can spread out and have

---

[93] cf. e.g. "How to Leverage Social Media for Public Relations Success" (eBook),
      http://www.hubspot.com/Portals/53/docs/hubspot_social_media_pr_ebook.pdf
[94] cf. e.g. "Predicting Box Office Results Using Twitter",
      http://cdn3.visibletechnolog.netdna-cdn.com/wp-
      content/uploads/2011/07/CS_Traditional-Research.pdf
[95] cf. e.g. "The Role of Social Media in Complaints Management",
      http://socialmediatoday.com/kimberly-kingsley/478388/role-social-media-complaints-
      management

harmful effects on reputation. A customer service team can monitor social media and decide whether complaints from customers should be ignored or responded to. Adding an influence metric, like the one provided by Klout, can be a factor to support this decision. Customer service would then concentrate on interactions with those customers where they expect the greatest positive effect on the corporate brand.

5.5   Information Diffusion

The combination of *social and technical* aspects that shape social networks make it worthwhile from a scientific standpoint to examine how exactly information does travel across such a network. The term *information diffusion* is frequently used, referring to the "dynamics of information propagation in environments of low-overhead personal publishing"[96] (like social networks). The underlying theories draw upon on scientific areas as diverse as epidemics, technological innovation, and game theory.

For example, it seems rewarding to analyze how the most influential *spreaders* can be identified in complex networks, because it promises insights into the patterns with which "people meet, ideas are spread and infectious diseases propagate"[97]. It has been suggested that, contrary to common belief, the 'best' spreaders are not always those people who generally are the most connected or most central within the network, i.e. possessing the largest numbers of connections. Instead, mathematical graph theory can be used to decompose the network and identify those nodes (i.e., in a social network, individuals) possessing the highest *k-cell index* within the network's graph[98].

Practical evidence seems to confirm that there are indeed other factors besides the mere number of connections that determine the effectiveness with which new information is spreading and traveling across a network. Authority, trust and persuasiveness of the individual spreading or relaying the news appear to be equally important. When U.S. Special Forces in

---

[96] according to [Gruh04]
[97] cf. [Kits10]
[98] see [Mior10], Fig. 1

Pakistan killed Osama Bin Laden in May 2011, for example, the news of his death spread widely and rapidly across social media. One such tweet[99] seems to have played an especially pivotal role in propagating the news. As one comprehensive analysis of Twitter traffic on that particular day reveals, "not even the smartest of machine learning algorithms could have predicted [the source's] online relevancy score, or his potential to spark an incredibly viral information flow. [...] His previous interactions and size and nature of his social graph did little to reflect his potential to generate thousands of people's willingness to trust within a matter of minutes."[100]

That said, it should now seem very promising to examine the stream of messages on a microblog. Ideally, it might be possible to assess how those employee contributions, individually and collectively, can be evaluated in order to obtain insights into the levels of authority, trust and persuasiveness of the individuals engaging in those conversations.

---

[99] https://twitter.com/#!/keithurbahn/status/64877790624886784
[100] see http://blog.socialflow.com/post/5246404319/breaking-bin-laden-visualizing-the-power-of-a-single

6   The Data Set

The data set that provides the basis for this research was derived from an actual, practical, corporate implementation of microblogging. The corporation, an investment bank with presences in over 70 countries globally, used an open-source microblogging solution[101] in an experimental pilot implementation to test new approaches to virtual teamwork, knowledge management, employee communities and internal collaboration. The microblog was made accessible via an intranet web site, reachable to employees in the information technology (IT) organization. Access and usage were restricted within the firewalls of the corporation, with no external visibility or interfaces to the Internet.

The solution relies on an underlying mySQL database to store all of its information, like users' profiles[102] and contributions. A replica of this database[103] was the foundation for the following analyses.

As the pilot implementation was rolled out, 24,457 individuals were identified (mostly based on their affiliation with the IT organization), invited to use the platform, and automatically registered, so that they are now users of the platform (i.e. the platform maintains a user profile for them). Of those, 4,826 distinct individuals (approx. 19.7%) have posted at least one status message (called a *notice*). Because in some cases the platform has posted system-generated automatic notices[104], the count of "real" platform users has to be corrected further: 2,575 distinct individuals (approx. 10.6%) have actively posted at least one personal notice and can be called *active users* or *adopters* of the solution.

Geographical distribution of contributors has not been within the scope of this analysis. An examination of contributions to another social software

---

[101] http://status.net/
[102] a user's profile consists of a short unique name (nickname), a picture, a short biography (300 characters) and a link to the official organizational employee directory
[103] obtained as a full database dump dating from May 3rd 2012; the respective SQL-DML/DDL script encompasses approx. 209 MBytes (uncompressed)
[104] in the form of "[username] has #joined [the platform]"

platform in 2011 by the same corporation showed that the majority of participants were located in the U.S. (approx. 24.4%), U.K. (23.4%) or Germany (15.4%). By analogy, it can be assumed that the microblog's population follows a similar distribution.

The following sections of this chapter will introduce some terminology: on *notices* (6.1), *subscriptions* (6.2), *favorites* (6.3), *repeats* (6.4), *replies* (6.5), *hashtags* (6.6) and *group memberships* (6.7). All these terms describe distinct features of the microblogging platform used. Examining those features and the respective slices of the data set, it will be possible to judge how well adopted those features have become by the community of contributors.

And finally, knowledge of these terms will be helpful as we assess whether the data set can actually be used as a basis for measuring an individual employee's activity or engagement on the platform as input for an incentive system.

6.1 Notices

The inaugural notice on the platform, being the first item in the data set, dates from May 18th 2010. The most recent notice is dated May 3rd 2012. Consequentially, this analysis spans almost two years' worth of data.

In total, 51,111 notices have been posted, an average of approx. 19.8 notices per active user as defined above. The most active individual has posted 2,496 notices.

The busiest day was December 15th 2010 with a total of 763 notices posted. On that day, a promotional *flash mob*[105] was organized, intended to promote usage of the platform, calling on the community of contributors for especially intense participation. On several other days with unusually high platform activity (February 24th 2011, March 21st 2011, July 28th 2011), enthusiasts accompanied internal organizational gatherings, like townhall meetings or house fairs, by *liveblogging*[106] on the social

---

[105] see http://en.wikipedia.org/wiki/Flash_mob
[106] see http://en.wikipedia.org/wiki/Liveblogging

software platform from their mobile devices. Discounting Saturdays and Sundays, but counting holidays (because of the global user base), there was an average of approx. 98.5 notices per working day.

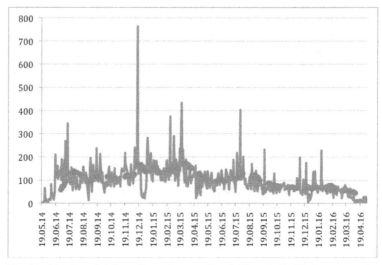

Fig. 12: Timeline of daily notice volume on the platform (with 30-day average)

The corporation is currently decommissioning the dedicated microblogging platform in favor of a newly implemented corporate collaboration solution that replaces the various platforms used for collaborative writing (wiki), discussions (forum), blogging and microblogging. The new solution has been designed and tested since October 2011 with a largely overlapping audience compared to the population examined by this research. The new solution was widely announced and made generally available in April 2012. At the same time, usage of the existing dedicated microblogging platform has been discouraged. This might serve to explain why the number of notice on the dedicated microblogging service has degraded over the past months.

6.2 Subscription and the Timeline

While it is theoretically permissible for a user of a microblog to read all the notices posted by everyone on the platform, this is probably a very rare use case. Most participants would certainly be overwhelmed by the

frequency of notices and will, instead, set up a personal selection of individuals who contribute content that is somewhat relevant to their work
tasks.

The platform supports this concentration of information and lets its users
choose which other individuals to *subscribe* to – in analogy to Twitter's
mechanism of *following*[107]. As a result, each user of the microblog sees
what is called a *personal timeline*: a chronological stream of messages
from individuals whose notices the user chose to follow[108].

Fig. 13: A user's "personal timeline" on the corporate microblog platform

Because each member of the platform may freely decide whom to follow,
the number of subscribers per individual varies widely and is certainly
interesting to observe from an analytical standpoint. It could provide an
insight with regards to who is posting content that is seen as relevant by
a number of others.

---

[107] https://support.twitter.com/articles/14019-what-is-following
[108] consequentially, it is then also possible to remove contributions from the personal
timeline by *unsubscribing* (or *unfollowing*) previously followed individuals

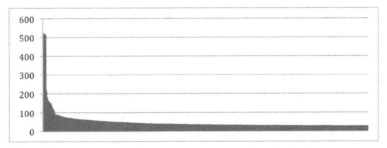

Fig. 14: Subscribers per individual, ordered by number of subscribers

The most followed individual in the data set examined has a total number of 507 subscribers reading their notices. There are 11 users with 100 or more subscribers, 41 accounts have at least 50 subscribers. And there are over 565 individuals (approx. 21.9% of active users) who have ten or more regular followers consuming the content they create or share.

6.3   Favorites

When users find notices in their personal timeline particularly interesting or useful, it costs them only a single click of the mouse to mark a notice as a *favorite*[109]. As a consequence, the original author of the message will be notified[110]: having a piece of information *favorited* by someone else is seen as recognition of one's contribution[111]. This feature effectively implements one of the very basic characteristics of a social software system: making it easy for participants to interact with the content generated by other individuals[112].

Within the data set examined for this analysis, the *favorite* feature was invoked 12,444 times. A total number of 8,075 distinct notices was *favorited* (approx. 15.8% of total notices).

---

[109] Facebook has recently made the term "like" very popular, with the now famous Facebook "like button" doing essentially the same;
see https://developers.facebook.com/docs/reference/plugins/like/
[110] http://status.net/wiki/Documentation#favorites
[111] see also https://support.twitter.com/articles/14214-about-favorites
[112] cf. [Koch09], p. 4

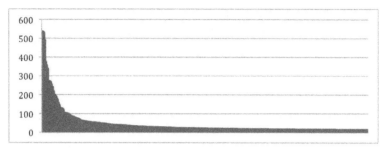

Fig. 15: Usage of the "favorite" feature per user, ordered by volume

The individual participant making the most active use of this feature *favorited* a total of 527 notices. 21 contributors to the microblogging service *favorited* at least 100 distinct notices. 203 distinct individuals (approx. 7.9%) made use of the *favorite* feature ten or more times. Overall, 1,235 distinct individuals (approx. 47.8%) made use of the *favorite* feature at least once.

It can thus be said that use of this feature was fairly widespread on the microblogging platform[113].

6.4 Repeats

Another possibility for users of the microblogging service to interact with notices appearing in their personal timeline is to *repeat* them[114]. A *repeat* of a notice will then propagate this particular piece of information into the personal timelines of the user's subscribers[115], even if they don't follow the original author of the contribution[116].

Like a *favorite* (6.3), a repeat requires only one single mouse click. This simplicity and ease of use makes the *repeat* feature very powerful and is a strong example for the effective *diffusion of information* in a social network (see 5.5).

---

[113] although it has to be said that no scientific research on a similar scale is known to the author that would allow putting these figures into perspective
[114] see http://status.net/wiki/Repeat
[115] on Twitter, this feature is called "retweet",
see https://support.twitter.com/articles/20169873-how-to-retweet-a-tweet
[116] see https://support.twitter.com/articles/77606-faqs-about-retweets-rt

Within the data set examined, platform participants have applied the *repeat* feature 505 times, thereby propagating a total number of 461 distinct notices (approx. .9% of total notices).

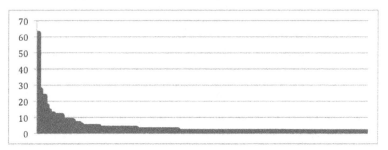

Fig. 16: Usage of the "repeat" feature per user, ordered by volume

One individual has *repeated* 62 distinct notices, but only 12 participants (approx. .5% of the population) have made use of the *repeat* feature ten or more times. 152 distinct individuals (approx. 5.9%) have used the *repeat* feature at least once.

Compared to the frequency with which the *favorite* feature was used, these numbers seem comparably low. It must be assumed that the *repeat* feature wasn't widely known, or has been adopted with restraint by platform participants for any other reason.

6.5   Replies

While *favorites* (6.3) and *repeats* (6.4) are used by subscribers to propagate interesting or relevant pieces of information across the community, the *reply* feature[117] can be used to engage two (or more) individuals in a two-way (or n-way) dialog[118]. Any notice appearing in a participant's personal timeline can be responded to, simply by clicking on the corresponding link to invoke the feature. The response will in turn appear in the original author's personal timeline, so that a conversation can take place. This feature is frequently used in problem solving use cases, e.g. to provide answers to questions posted or to ask for clarification.

---

[117] see http://status.net/wiki/Documentation#replies
[118] see also https://support.twitter.com/articles/14023-what-are-replies-and-mentions

19,568 notices contained in the data set were *replies* in reaction to a pre-ceding notice from someone else (approx. 38.3%). Looking at the same context differently, 15,745 of the notices contained in the data set went answered or followed up by someone else's reply (approx. 30.8%).

The most active participant has provided a total number of 888 *replies* to notices from other users of the platform. 46 distinct contributors have each generated at least 100 conversational replies. 247 participants (ap-prox. 9.6% of the population) have replied to contributions at least ten times, and a total number of 1,183 distinct individuals (approx. 45.8%) have used the reply feature at least once.

These numbers, overall, seem to suggest a relatively high level of collec-tive engagement.

6.6 Hashtags

Hashtags are a means of categorizing notices, functioning like keywords. The # (*hash*) symbol is used to prefix a word in a notice; that word will then be interpreted by the platform as a keyword or topic. The idea "was created organically by Twitter users"[119].

The idea has become generally accepted and very popular on Twitter to bring some organic, self-organized structure in the seemingly cluttered, constantly flowing and otherwise strictly chronological stream of mes-sages[120]: Words denoted as hashtags will become clickable. If a user clicks on a hashtag, the platform will automatically bring up a search page, listing all notices that contain this particular hashtag. Scientific or industry conferences, for example, often promote an *official hashtag*; at-tendees will mark their tweets accordingly. It then becomes possible for everyone to follow the proceedings of the conference by filtering the Twitter stream and using that particular hashtag[121].

---

[119] see also https://support.twitter.com/entries/49309-what-are-hashtags-symbols
[120] see http://www.newyorker.com/online/blogs/susanorlean/2010/06/hash.html
[121] see http://nextconf.eu/next11/getting-ready-for-next11/

Hashtags carry semantics: The concept can be used to express positive sentiment (*#like*, *#thanks*), but they can also be used for criticism or failure (*#fail*[122]).

The concept has obviously been understood and applied by a significant number of users of the corporate microblog: Among the 51,111 notices contained in the data set, 24,530 (or approx. 48.0%) contained at least one *hashtag*. 1,319 distinct individuals (approx. 51.1%) have published at least one notice that contained a *hashtag*.

6.7   Group Memberships

The software used as a basis for the corporate microblogging platform also provides a *group* feature. This feature takes the subscription functionality introduced above (6.2) from the individual to the collective level: It allows subscribing to a group of participants rather than any contributor individually. The functionality seems to be modeled after Twitter's popular *list* feature[123]: All messages posted to the group (by any member, or even by a non-member) will then appear in the personal *timelines* of any group subscriber.

While the contributors to the corporate microblogging platform examined herein have made extensive use of this feature (they formed a total number of 571 groups, the largest having 386 members), group memberships have not been examined as part of this research.

6.8   Examples

Before coming to the conclusion of this chapter, let us look at two subsets of the data examined that seem to illustrate rather well how the basic, atomic functions of the microblog (*notices*, *replies*, *repeats*) can be used for effective information diffusion and problem-solving conversations.

---

[122] see http://hashtags.org/fail
[123] see https://support.twitter.com/articles/76460-how-to-use-twitter-lists

In the first example, an employee (user ID 459551) announces a pilot implementation for a novel kind of software platform. He defines an impromptu *hashtag* and calls for participation. Although his number of subscribers is fairly low, his message is amplified by three *repeats* within less than 24 hours. Another individual (user ID 23561) asks a question about this initiative and receives an answer within just over two hours from another colleague (user ID 58081). The two enter a short dialog that goes back and forth a couple of times before coming to a positive resolution.

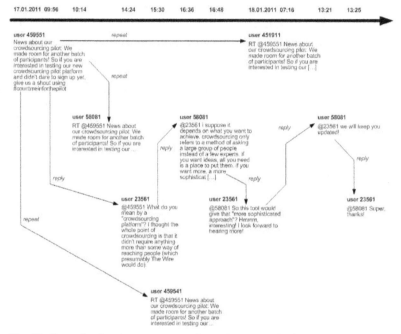

Fig. 17: Example of notice propagation: "crowdsourcing pilot"

In the other example, an employee (user ID 50711) announces the schedule to migrate the corporate e-mail and collaboration solution to a new product platform. Recognized by subscribers as widely relevant information, the notice is *repeated* three times within just over twelve hours. Four individuals (user IDs 62131, 191181, 192031, 200001) respond with questions regarding timing of the migration in their specific office locations. The original contributor responds to three of the four questions, apparently resolving two of them. One of those answers triggers a follow-up question from another colleague (user ID 48531) that is finally resolved by the original contributor pointing to an intranet website with further information on the migration project's timelines.

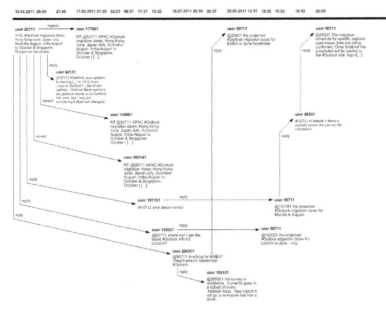

Fig. 18: Example of notice propagation: "e-mail migration"

6.9   Interpretations

Readers looking at this data set from the viewpoints of social media enthusiasts may at first be disillusioned: Very large numbers of users seem
to be *lurkers* – individuals who may be visiting the platform, but stay
passive, with apparently no significant contributions. The *inner circle* of
productive users on the platform appears to be very small. This observation may be true, but is hardly surprising at closer examination: Concluding this chapter, let us look at two studies to put our observations into
perspective.

Firstly, research by the Norman Nielsen Group has shown that in traditional internet-based *communities* (newsgroups, discussion forums), 90%
of users remain passive, 7% contribute reactively to content previously
provided by others, but only 3% of the population actively contribute to
the community. While social-software-based communities have significantly increased the level of active participation to 8%, and the share of
reactive contributions to 32%, the majority of individuals (60%) still remain passive altogether.[124] The sample contained in this data set only
seems to confirm this distribution fundamentally.

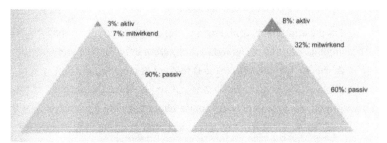

Fig. 19: Active/reactive/passive users, before and after social software[125]

Secondly, the distribution of content contribution across the user base
seems supportive of an Internet-age phenomenon that has been de-

---

[124] cf. [Dörf12], p. 27
[125] diagram taken from [Dörf12], p. 27

scribed as *the long tail*[126]. Internet businesses, like Amazon or eBay, can sell a vast variety of items in relatively small quantities each. Traditionally, niche products or content would have been 'hidden' in the depth of the long tail, but the advanced possibilities of information diffusion and filter-based selection have allowed this kind of content distribution to function effectively.

Put differently and placed in the context of this research, it does not play a decisive role whether a social software contributor has five or fifty subscribers. If contributions are relevant, even within a small group, they can be immensely valuable. Furthermore, information diffusion mechanisms can amplify content so that it reaches a wider audience (e.g. via *repeats*) as soon as it is considered to be of broader relevance.

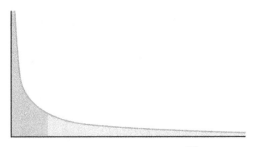

Fig. 20: "Long tail" curve characteristic[127]

Thirdly and finally, it seems an interesting observation that the microblogging features *reply* and *favorite* were used so frequently in comparison to the equally powerful *repeat* feature. Examining microblog adoption on a feature-by-feature basis was not required for the purpose of this research, so we can only speculate about possible reasons: Maybe the *reply* and *favorite* features are more accepted because they resemble mechanisms known from more established technologies (e.g. e-mail and Facebook), while the *repeat* feature is unique to microblogging and hence probably less known.

---

[126] cf. [Ande08]
[127] http://en.wikipedia.org/wiki/File:Long_tail.svg

7 Analysis, Measurements and Scoring

Within this chapter, the data set will be analyzed for metrics that can be included as factors in an employee incentive system. For the analysis to be targeted and purposeful, we will firstly make an attempt to state *desired behaviors*. Ideally, the degree of compliance with these intended behaviors can then be measured on an individual basis.

7.1 Desired Behaviors

Our study is attempting to provide a systemic link between corporate strategy and individual employee behavior. But what are the specific behaviors expected of the employees who are using a social software platform? If we were to use scoring that follows this analysis in an employee incentive system, we should focus on those individual behaviors that are explicitly *desired*.

In order to accomplish this, a very small, informal survey among eight employees was used. All of the respondents were familiar with the basic principles of the microblog, but not all of them were active users. Some were managers, others individual contributors.

Four degrees of system usage were jointly defined – listed here, from weakest to strongest intensity:

1. Regular visits to the platform to learn, find solutions for work problems, get to know people or navigate the organization.
2. Frequency of active contributions to the platform (notices posted).
3. Frequency of interaction with contributions from other individuals (e.g. in the form of *replies*, *repeats*, *favorites*).
4. Quality of interaction and contributions as seen by the peers in the community (e.g. based on *favorites* or certain *hashtags*)

Visits to the platform (number 1. above), although desirable, could not be examined within the scope of this analysis. This research was based only on contributions. Web site analytics (see 4.3) were not be taken into account.

The survey group further concluded that putting too much emphasis on the *frequency* of microblog notices and the *intensity* of contributions (number 2. above) would provide misleading incentives to the individual: users who are simply *talkative* aren't automatically seen as particularly *helpful* or *useful*. Consequentially, such behavior shouldn't be encouraged *per se*. One survey participant notably mentioned that behaviors desired on the managerial level may differ from those desired of individual contributors. This might be an interesting topic for further research (see 8.4).

Wherever there was *correspondence and dialog* among individuals (number 3. above), i.e. questions asked or arguments clarified, the related contributions were seen as useful to the corporation. The group proposed the consideration of *replies* as components of a metric expressing a desired behavior.

The *quality* of individual contributions, expressed by *peer feedback* (4.) gained the strongest support from the group of respondents and is hence the most desired behavior. It was concluded that *repeats of* and *favorites for* an individual's contributions were highly indicative of quality. The group proposed the inclusion of these mechanisms as components of a metric expressing a clearly desired behavior.

The metric describing these most desired behaviors – correspondence and quality – could be termed *usefulness* or *utility*.

Secondly, members of the group advocated the introduction of an *influence* (or *connectedness*) metric, similar to the concept applied by Klout (see 5.1). This would support the intended *diffusion of information* across the social network, discourage isolation and emphasize the strategic ambition to facilitate *informal employee-to-employee relationships* across corporate divisions and at all levels of the corporate hierarchy. It was concluded that the *number of subscribers* could be significant in this respect, in analogy to print media *reach* as a success factor. On a microblog, going a step further, the static number of subscribers (measuring *reach*) can be seen in combination with more dynamic factors (audience reactions) to potentially measure and individual's *influence*.

7.2   The "#platformwin" Hashtag

As we saw in the first examination of the data set above (6.6), microblog contributors can use *hashtags* as keywords classifyin notices. A very insightful example of this phenomenon was observed in the data set during this research: the community had introduced a *#platformwin* hashtag to recognize especially helpful contributions. When one individual *A* posted a question to the microblogging community and another individual *B* responded with a helpful answer, it became customary for *A* to acknowledge the contribution and round off the dialog with a final notice expressing thankfulness (e.g. "that solved my problem, thanks"). Including this particular hashtag (*#platformwin*) in the notice indicates that finding a solution without the microblogging platform might have been difficult or even impossible.

Obviously, not every individual was aware of this convention, and many cases can be found in the data set where a substantial contribution was not recognized in this manner. Still, occurrences of this particular hashtag are helpful in measuring the quality of contributions from microblog participants.

7.3   Observations

The data set was queried using the SQL language, mining for insightful information on a user-by-user basis. After some analysis, the following atomic criteria crystallized that seemed to allow quantitative and qualitative measurements of contributions made by an individual X.

Symbol	Definition, description
S	Total number of other individuals who are subscribers to X
N	Total number of notices posted by X
RE_{in}	Total number of direct replies X has received (inbound) from other individuals
RE_{ou}	Total number of direct replies X has posted (outbound) in response to other individuals
RP_{in}	Total number of notices X has repeated that were originally posted by other individuals (inbound)
RP_{ou}	Total number of notices X has posted (outbound) that were subsequently repeated by other individuals, e.g. his subscribers
FV_{in}	Total number of favorites X has expressed for notices originally posted by other individuals (inbound)

Symbol	Definition, description
FV_{ou}	Total number of favorites X has received for notices X originally posted (outbound)
HT_{in}	Total number of notices with a "#platformwin" hashtag X has posted, reacting to and recognizing contributions received from other individuals (inbound)
HT_{ou}	Total number of "#platformwin" hashtags X has received from subscribers in responses to notices X originally posted (outbound)

Table 1:   Atomic criteria as components for scoring contributions

7.4   Sample Group Selection

A sample group of twelve individuals was identified and selected from the total population of contributors to the microblog platform. These individuals were not chosen randomly, but with some consideration, e.g. purposefully picking one individual with a relatively high number of notices posted and a relatively low number of subscribers (user ID 450791), and another one, vice versa, with a low number of notices posted to a comparably high number of subscribers (user ID 212921).

User ID	S	N	RE_{in}	RE_{ou}	RP_{in}	RP_{ou}	FV_{in}	FV_{ou}	HT_{in}	HT_{ou}
41	210	2,404	1037	865	59	44	772	511	24	23
61	173	691	281	395	3	7	167	360	2	3
111	507	1,088	540	435	4	19	544	256	2	17
12661	56	285	92	129	1	2	139	126	2	0
40401	13	10	5	3	0	0	1	4	0	0
48531	18	290	167	235	0	0	83	30	3	0
177691	152	296	146	173	23	5	50	35	7	2
212921	154	118	67	30	0	5	125	14	1	0
375281	72	623	333	511	1	3	113	175	6	2
450771	134	951	287	387	12	6	165	329	3	19
450791	46	1,095	521	612	6	9	148	484	19	39
450841	64	343	126	145	10	9	74	52	0	10

Table 2:   Sample group (n=12) used for scoring verification

This sample group was later used to test the metrics derived from the data set.

7.5   Influence Metric (INF)

Based on the considerations above defining desired behaviors, the number of *subscribers per individual* (S) was used as an expression of the individual's influence across the network. Further factors to determine the *influence metric* (INF) over a distinct time period are:

- usage of the *repeat* feature by the individual (RP_{in}) and by their peers in recognition of contributions (RP_{ou}), acknowledging the importance of information diffusion
- notices written as *responses* (RE_{ou}) and notices *received* as responses (RE_{in}), assuming that conversations are influential and emphasizing the desirability of employee-to-employee dialog.

The following formula resulted from these considerations:

$$INF := \frac{\ln(S) \cdot \left(RP_{in} + RP_{ou} + RE_{in} + RE_{ou}\right)}{10}$$

Please note that the number of *subscribers per individual* (S) was assigned a weight on a logarithmic scale. This was intended to limit the incentive provided to individuals who simply collect subscribers to improve their score. An individual *B* with 1,000 subscribers should not score ten times higher than another individual *A* with 100 subscribers. The logarithmic scale reduces *B*'s advantage to a factor of *e* instead of ten.

7.6   Utiliy Metric (UTI)

Attempting to judge the *usefulness* (or *utility*) of contributions made by any employee to the corporate microblog, the *number of subscribers* (S) was disregarded entirely. Instead, the following components were weighted and taken into account to determine an individual's *utility score* (UTI) over a distinct time period:

- notices written as *responses* (RE_{ou}) and notices received as responses (RE_{in}), again, assuming that conversations are influential and emphasizing the desirability of employee-to-employee dialog
- usage of the *repeat* feature by the individual (RP_{in}) and by their peers in recognition of contributions (RP_{ou}), again, recognizing the importance of information diffusion
- usage of the *favorite* feature by the individual (FV_{in}) and by their peers in reaction to their notices (FV_{ou}) as a qualitative measure of contribution quality
- usage of the *#platformwin* hashtag by the individual in recognition of other's contributions (HT_{in}) and by their peers in reaction to their

contributions (HT_{ou}) as a qualitative measure of contribution quality.

Based on these criteria, the following formula was derived:

$$UTI := \frac{RE_{ou} + RE_{in} + 3 \times RP_{in} + 6 \times RP_{ou} + 3 \times FV_{in} + 6 \times FV_{ou} + 6 \times HT_{in} + 12 \times HT_{ou}}{10}$$

Weightings were used to emphasize features that, while rarely used, clearly express contribution *quality* over mere quantity (*repeats*, *favorites* and the *#platformwin* hashtag).

The total *number of notices posted by an individual* (N) was explicitly not considered to be a helpful metric. Instead, based on the above definition of desired behaviors, the number of *replies* posted and *replies* received were taken into consideration. This practice effectively discounts notices that were mere broadcasts (neither responded to nor a response to someone else's message).

7.7   Composite Incentive Score (CIS)

Combining the metrics for *influence* (INF) and *utility* (UTI) per individual, a *composite incentive score* (CIS) for any given time period can be computed as follows:

$$CIS := .3 \times INF + .7 \times UTI$$

The relatively strong weighting of UTI shall express the significance of making contributions that are seen as *useful* by peers in the organization, tying the score back to the desired behaviors defined as the basis for this analysis (7.1). At the same time, the comparably low weighting of INF diminishes the effect of the mere number of relationships, while still expressing the growth of one's professional network and the desirability of informal employee-to-employee relationships as secondary objectives.

7.8   Examples

To verify the scoring algorithms and provide additional insights, let us look at two examples from the data sample and visualize how their scoring evolved over time along with varying degrees of intensity using the microblogging platform.

One user's total incentive score over the entire observation period was 32.6. He scored a maximum of 61.5 *composite incentive points* (CIS) in May 2011 – based, among other factors, on 70 received *favorites*, two *#platformwin* hashtags received and six of his contributions *repeated*, resulting in the highest monthly UTI score derived from the data set (UTI=60.6). The total *number of notices posted* (N) during that month was 172, which is interesting because there were two months with higher notice volumes but resulting in significantly lower utility and incentive scores (July 2010: N=178, INF=96.3, UTI=27.9, CIS=48.4; February 2011: N=179, INF=78.1, UTI=43.2, CIS=53.7).

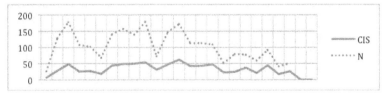

Fig. 21: Monthly notice volume and incentive score (user ID 41)

Another user has obviously adopted the platform relatively late in its life cycle. Summoning only 18 *subscribers*, he was still able to score 14.5 *composite incentive points* in January 2012, based on just 43 notices (N=43, INF=16.8, UTI=13.5).

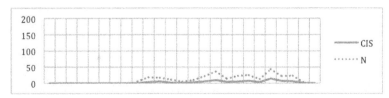

Fig. 22: Monthly notice volume and incentive score (user ID 48531)

7.9 Scoring Results

Applying the algorithms described above for INF, UTI and CIS scoring, the contributions made by the individuals contained in the data sample result in the following evaluation.

User ID	S	N	INF	UTI	CIS
41	210	2,404	42.9	28.1	32.6
61	173	691	14.1	8.7	10.3
111	507	1,088	24.9	17.1	19.5
12661	56	285	3.6	5.0	4.6
40401	13	10	.1	.1	.1
48531	18	290	4.6	2.5	3.1
177691	152	296	7.0	2.4	3.8
212921	154	118	2.1	3.3	3.0
375281	72	623	14.5	5.2	8.0
450771	134	951	13.6	8.8	10.2
450791	46	1,095	13.6	11.5	13.3
450841	64	343	4.8	3.0	3.5

Table 3:   Results for INF, UTI and INC scoring

Scores have been rounded to a single decimal.

7.10 Examination of Correlations

Rounding off the analysis, it should be interesting to examine how the *incentive score* (CIS) correlates with the number *of subscribers* (S) and the *number of notices* (N), respectively. Using Pearson's coefficient, the following correlations can be determined:

$r_{CIS,N} = .9796$

$r_{CIS,S} = .5727$

There is also a remarkable correlation between the *influence* (INF) and *utility* (UTI) components of the CIS:

$r_{INF,UTI} = .9693$

8   Summary

8.1   Research Methods

Literature study and Internet research provided the basis for the intro-
ductory chapters on social software (2), corporate change management
(3), conventional media (4) and social software analysis (5).

The subsequent empirical analysis of the data set at hand (as described
in chapters 6 and 7) consisted of the following steps:

1. A database dump was obtained. The mySQL database had supported a corporate implementation of microblogging. The data set
   consisted of 51,111 notices posted by 2,582 distinct individuals
   who posted at least one notice manually. Notices contained in the
   data set covered a timeframe from May 2010 to May 2012.
2. SQL queries were used to explore the database schema on a feature-by-feature basis, analyzing the general acceptance per feature among the community of platform participants.
3. Based on a small informal survey, two desired employee behaviors
   were identified and described: *utility* and *influence*.
   Those behaviors became the basis for further analysis towards
   metrics that might contribute to an employee incentive system.
4. Several atomic metrics were defined, each expressing an isolated
   aspect of individual behavior on the microblogging platform,
   e.g. the number of notices or the use of certain features.
5. A sample group of twelve user profiles was selected, intended to
   provide a reasonably sized testing ground for metrics.
6. Based on an analysis with the sample group of twelve users, metrics for the *utility* of contributions and the *influence* of the individual were defined. The two metrics were combined into one composite incentive score.
7. All three metrics were calculated and presented for the entire sample group.

8. The analysis concluded by describing how the components of the incentive score correlate with primary parameters contained in the data set.

8.2 Summarization of Findings

It can be concluded that the stream of notices contained in the microblog data set provides a variety of factors that can be taken into account as metrics for employee behavior and provide a basis for an incentive system. The nature of microblogging – short text messages that propagate across a network by means of very elementary mechanisms, like *subscription*, *repeats* or *responses* – seems very well suited for such an analysis. Based on a previous statement of desired employee behavior, it was possible to extract two metrics – describing an employees' *influence* across the network and the *utility* of their contributions as recognized by peers. These two factors could be combined in a single numerical score. Such scoring can be used as input to an employee incentive system intended to reward extraordinarily active or useful contributions.

Summing up: The thesis defining this research could clearly be verified.

8.3 Critique

Several concerns have manifested over the course of this research that need to be presented for a balanced treatment of the subject matter. They can be grouped in three areas: (1) legal and privacy concerns, (2) the research method and tools used and (3) the general suitability of employee performance indicators.

Concerns relating to *legal and privacy aspects* arise from the fact that all correspondence on microblogging platforms is openly visible for everyone. As one source recognizes, "protecting privacy is a legal requirement, based [e.g.] on European Union Directive 95/46/EC"[128], so unless this situation is addressed by corporate governance policies, individual employees could refuse usage of the platform altogether. In Germany, spe-

---

[128] [Bege10]

cifically, applicable law states that a workers' council has co-determina-
tion rights on business decisions concerning the "introduction and usage
of technical equipment intended to supervise worker's behavior or performance"[129] – this would clearly apply to an incentive system based on
social software contributions. To address these concerns effectively, it
may be required to formulate the incentive system in a way that makes
participation in microblogging purely voluntary. The incentive system
would then have to state that while extraordinary contributions to the
microblog will be recognized or rewarded, the absence thereof must
never justify any negative judgment.

Furthermore, several restrictions relating to the *research method and
tools* seem to be limiting the validity of this analysis:

- The *number of subscribers* (S) metric was only available as of May
  2012 in the data set with no historical information, so changes to
  an individual's subscriber base could not be evaluated over time.
- Analytical tools were limited to mySQL, SQL queries and Microsoft
  Excel. Due to the absence of a programming language in the tool
  set, it was not possible to calculate the influence metric recursively[130]. This might have provided interesting results.
- There were some system-generated notices in the data set that
  were not posted by human users. While precautions were taken to
  discount those, the method may not have discounted all such messages. This might have diluted analysis results.
- The sample population used to test the scoring algorithm was limited to twelve individuals to allow manual computation. Using a
  programming language to calculate scores automatically, a larger
  population could have been tested.
- Evaluating usage of *#platformwin* hashtags provided valuable insight, but there were other hashtags (*#thanks*, *#win*) that were
  not recognized by the scoring algorithm.

---

[129] BetrVG §87 (1) 6., see http://www.gesetze-im-internet.de/betrvg/__87.html;
author's translation
[130] Klout, for example, recursively draws its scoring on the influence scores for all members within an individual's network

- The scoring may under-represent specific use cases for professional microblogging. For example, members of a project team posting daily status updates[131] might have a limited *number of subscribers* and lowly numbers of *responses* to notices. Using the scoring proposed above, they would score relatively low despite actively using the platform purposefully within a smaller community and perfectly supportive of organizational goals.

- The correlation between both scoring components and the *number of contributions from an individual* (N) might hint at a deficiency of the algorithm: being "talktative" was expressly not a desired behavior.

The last two points, especially, may lead to a broader critique of the *suitability of performance indicators* in judgment of human behavior. It is generally difficult to model desired behaviors so that the right indicators will be extracted from the variety of possibilities in any given data set[132]. It has been pointed out that extrinsic motivation – like the motivation provided by an employee incentive system – "may actually reduce or crowd out intrinsic motivation"[133], leading to unintended or even adverse effects. Finally, discussing employee incentive systems and social software, one source pointed out the risk that "such a tool can also create an incentive for users to change their actions in order to improve how they are reflected in the tool, that is, to *game* the system".

Concluding this critique, it can be reemphasized that this analysis was indeed successful in providing a *qualitative* measurement of employee activity on the social software platform. However, it must be noted that desired employee behavior can only be expressed within the context of a precisely stated corporate strategy. Corporate strategy was not considered during this research, so it remains unclear whether the composite incentive score (CIS) actually provides the *right* incentives for successful strategic alignment.

---

[131] cf. [Adle11]
[132] cf. [Fitz96]
[133] [Kapl96], p. 221

8.4 Topics for Further Research

Further research might therefore concentrate on bridging the gap between corporate strategic objectives and statements of desired behaviors that could be used to measure employee contributions accordingly. It should be very interesting to study how social software applications can be supportive of strategic alignment (according to Kaplan and Norton) based on empirical study with larger populations and ideally based on actual statements of corporate strategy, i.e. formulated in balanced scorecards.

During the informal survey used to formulate desired behaviors, a senior specialist for corporate communications and cultural change mentioned that it might be interesting to differentiate between the behaviors desired from *individual contributors* (usage of the medium to share what you know or ask questions) and *managers* or *corporate leaders* (usage of the medium to serve as role models, recognize contributions, provide strategic insights and solicit employee feedback). This may be a very rewarding area for more intensive research.

Relationships between contributors to the corporate microblogging platform become evident when examining the use of the *subscription* feature or analyzing the use of the *reply* feature to maintain dialog. This could provide an interesting basis for analytics of the corporation's *social graph* based on mathematical graph theory.

The literature review conducted during this research has surfaced an interesting method to detect the *spreading of rumors* in social media[134]. Since spreading rumors is most certainly an undesired professional behavior, it may be interesting in the future to see if this method can be applied to the stream of notices provided in a corporate microblog. The absence of rumors in an individual's contribution could turn out to be a *hygiene factor* in the objectives stated as leading to an employee's incentive score.

---

[134] [Qazv11]

Finally, a very interesting contemporary research area is how the virtual and physical worlds can be combined. *Augmented reality* applications are one example: they are location-aware and can enrich live images with contextual information, e.g. on a smartphone screen. But the principle works the other way, too: *Ambient media* researchers in Karlsruhe have designed an appliance that detects events in the virtual world and presents them "in our surrounding space in subtle [...] ways", in this case by controlling a fountain of water to visualize web site traffic (more traffic resulting in a higher fountain)[135].

Applying *ambient media* ideas to social software can go as far as dispensing bubblegum to microbloggers for every *retweet* or *favorite* of their contributions. It may sound crazy, but such an appliance has in fact already been built[136]. From a point of view of scientific curiosity, this idea should certainly be explored further.

---

[135] https://www.ibr.cs.tu-bs.de/users/beigl/publication/ambient.pdf
[136] http://ollyfactory.com/polly/

9   Bibliography and References

Abra04   Abras, Chadia; Maloney-Krichmar, Diane; Preece, Jenny; "User-Centered
          Design"; in "Encyclopedia of Human-Computer Interaction"
          (editor: Bainbridge, W.); Thousand Oaks: Sage Publications, 2004

Adle11   Adler, Jochen; "Microblogging im virtuellen Projektteam: Untersuchung der
          Eignung von Microblogging zur internen Projektkommunikation als effektive
          Alternative zur E-Mail"; Grin Publishing, 2011

Ande08   Anderson, Chris; "The Long Tail: Why The Future of Business Is Selling
          Less Of More"; Hyperion Books, 2008

Back08   Back, Andrea; Gronau, Norbert; Tochtermann, Klaus; „Web 2.0 in der
          Unternehmenspraxis – Grundlagen, Fallstudien und Trends zum Einsatz von
          Social Software"; Oldenbourg, 2008

Bege10   Begel, Andrew; DeLine, Robert; Zimmermann, Thomas; "Social Media for
          Software Engineering"; in "FoSER 10 Proceedings of the FSE/SDP workshop
          on Future of software engineering research", Association for Computing
          Machinery (ACM), New York, 2010

Belc96   Belcher, John G.; "How to Design & Implement a Results-Oriented Variable
          Pay System"; AMACOM American Management Association, 1996

Bugh11   Bughin, Jacques; Hung Byers, Angela; Chui, Michael; "How social
          technologies are extending the organization"; in: McKinsey Quarterly;
          November 2011; condensed form available online:
          http://www.mckinseyquarterly.com/High_Tech/Strategy_Analysis/
          How_social_technologies_are_extending_the_organization_2888

Buhs08   Buhse, Willms; Stamer, Sören (Eds.); „Die Kunst, loszulassen – Enterprise
          2.0"; Rhombos, 2008

Davi86   Davis, Fred D.; "A technology acceptance model for empirically testing new
          end-user information systems: theory and results"; Massachusetts Institute
          of Technology, Sloan School of Management, 1986; available online:
          http://hdl.handle.net/1721.1/15192

Dopp08   Doppler, Klaus; Lauterburg, Christoph; "Change Management – Den
          Unternehmenswandel gestalten"; 12th edition, Campus 2008

Dörf12   Dörfel, Lars; Schulz, Theresa (Eds.); "Social Media in der internen
          Kommunikation"; scm, prismus communications; 1st edition, Berlin, 2012

Druc56   Drucker, Peter F.; "Praxis des Managements";
          Econ Verlag; Düsseldorf, 1956

Fitz90   Fitz-Gibbon, Carol; "Performance Indicators"; Bera Dialogs No. 2;
          Multilingual Matters, 1990

Gruh04   Gruhl, D.; Liben-Nowell, David; Guha, R.; Tomkins, A.; "Information
           Diffusion Through Blogspace"; WWW2004 Conference; New York, 2004;
           available online: http://www2004.org/proceedings/docs/1p491.pdf

Günt09   Günther, Oliver; Krasnova, Hanna; Riehle, Dirk; Schoendienst, Valentin;
           "Modeling Microblogging Adoption in the Enterprise"; in: "AMCIS 2009
           Proceedings"; available online: http://aisel.aisnet.org/amcis2009/544

Hahn06   Hahn, Dietger; Taylor, Bernard (Eds.); „Strategische Unternehmensplanung
           – Strategische Unternehmensführung"; Springer, 9th edition, 2006

Java07   Java, Akshay; Song, Xiaodan; Finin, Tim; Tseng, Belle; „Why We Twitter:
           understanding microblogging usage and communities"; in „Proceedings of
           the 9th WebKDD and 1st SNA-KDD 2007 workshop on Web mining and
           social network analysis", 2007

Kapl96   Kaplan, Robert S.; Norton, David P.; "The Balanced Scorecard"; Harvard
           Business School Press; Boston, 1996

Kits10   Kitsak, Maksim; Gallos, Lazaros K.; Havlin, Shlomo; Liljeros, Fredrik;
           Muchnik, Lev; Stanley, H. Eugene; Makse, Hernán A.: "Identification of
           influential spreaders in complex networks"; Nature Physics, Volume 6,
           November 2010; available online: http://arxiv.org/pdf/1001.5285.pdf

Koch09   Koch, Michael; Richter, Alexander; „Enterprise 2.0 – Planung, Einführung
           und erfolgreicher Einsatz von Social Software in Unternehmen", 2nd edition,
           Oldenbourg, 2009

Kott96   Kotter, John P.; "Leading Change"; Harvard Business School Press, 1996

McAf09   McAfee, Andrew; „Enterprise 2.0 – New collaborative tools for your
           organization's toughest challenges"; Harvard Business Press, 2009

Mior10   Miorandi, Daniele; De Pellegrini, Francesco; "K-Shell Decomposition for
           Dynamic Complex Networks"; Proceedings of the WDN, 2010;
           available online:
           http://hal.inria.fr/docs/00/49/20/57/PDF/p499-miorandi.pdf

Naon08   Naone, Erica; „A Brief History Of Microblogging"; in „Technology Review",
           September/October 2008; available online:
           https://www.technologyreview.com/files/18810/forward.pdf

News10   Newsgator Technologies, "The Benefits of Microblogging in the Enterprise";
           available online:
           http://www.newsgator.com/LinkClick.aspx?fileticket=9skeL_2DMyg%3D

ORei05   O'Reilly, Tim; „What is Web 2.0"; available online:
           http://oreilly.com/web2/archive/what-is-web-20.html

Page04   Page, Lawrence; „Method for scoring documents in a linked database";
           Patent Nr. US6799176; available online, accessible via the European Patent
           Office: http://v3.espacenet.com/publicationDetails/biblio?CC=US&
           NR=6799176B1&KC=B1&FT=D&date=20040928

Pari11   Pariser, Eli; "The Filter Bubble: What The Internet Is Hiding From You";
           Penguin Books, 2011

Qazv11   Qazvinian, Vahed; Rosengren, Emily; Radev, Dragomir R.; Mei, Qiaozhu:
           "Rumor has it: Identifying Misinformation in Microblogs"; in: "Proceedings
           of the 2011 Conference on Empirical Methods in Natural Language
           Processing"; Edinburgh, Scotland, 2011

Rieg07   Riegner, Cate: "Word of Mouth on the Web: The Impact of Web 2.0 on
           Consumer Purchase Decisions"; in: "Journal of Advertising Research";
           December, 2007

Venk03   Venkatesh, Viswanath; Morris, Michael G.; Davis, Gordon B.; Davis, Fred
           D.: "User Acceptance of Information Technology: Toward a Unified View",
           in: "MIS Quarterly Vol. 27 No. 3", September 2003"; available online:
           http://citeseerx.ist.psu.edu/viewdoc/summary?doi=10.1.1.197.1486

All online sources, quoted as URLs in this bibliography or in footnotes, have been verified on May 17th 2012.

10 Appendix

10.1 SQL Queries

Symbol	SQL Query
S	SELECT "S", COUNT(subscriber) FROM subscription WHERE subscribed=@user
N	SELECT "N ", COUNT(id) FROM notice WHERE (profile_id=@user AND created>=@date1 AND created<=@date2)
RE_{in}	SELECT "REin", COUNT(id) FROM notice WHERE reply_to AND reply_to IN (SELECT id FROM notice WHERE profile_id=@user) AND created>=@date1 AND created<=@date2
RE_{ou}	SELECT "REou", COUNT(id) FROM notice WHERE reply_to AND profile_id=@user AND created>=@date1 AND created<=@date2
RP_{in}	SELECT "RPin", COUNT(id) FROM notice WHERE repeat_of AND profile_id=@user AND created>=@date1 AND created<=@date2
RP_{ou}	SELECT "RPou", COUNT(id) FROM notice WHERE repeat_of AND repeat_of IN (SELECT id FROM notice WHERE profile_id=@user) AND created>=@date1 AND created<=@date2
FV_{in}	SELECT "FVin", COUNT(notice_id) FROM fave WHERE user_id=@user AND modified>=@date1 AND modified<=@date2
FV_{ou}	SELECT "FVou", COUNT(fave.notice_id) FROM fave, notice WHERE fave.notice_id=notice.id AND notice.profile_id=@user AND notice.created>=@date1 AND notice.created<=@date2
HT_{ou}	SELECT "HTou", COUNT(id) FROM notice_tag, notice WHERE tag="platformwin" AND notice.id=notice_tag.notice_id AND profile_id=@user AND notice.created>@date1 AND notice.created<=@date2
HT_{in}	SELECT "HTin", COUNT(notice_id) FROM notice_tag, notice AS N, notice AS N2, profile WHERE tag = 'platformwin' AND N.id=notice_tag.notice_id AND N2.id=N.reply_to AND profile.id=N2.profile_id AND N2.profile_id=@user AND notice_tag.created>=@date1 AND notice_tag.created<=@date2

Table 4:   SQL Queries used to derive metrics used for scoring

The SQL variables *@user*, *@date1* and *@date2* were used as input parameters for the SQL queries.